GNOME ALONE
IN CARMEL

PUBLISHER
Seton Publishing • Carmel, California

ISBN-13: 978-0-9989605-4-8
Printed in the United States of America

PHOTOGRAPHS
John Firman, Ann Gila, Fred Nelson, Karyl Hall

BOOK DESIGN
Michelle Manos Design, Carmel, California

SETON
PUBLISHING

GNOME ALONE
IN CARMEL

Karyl Hall ♡

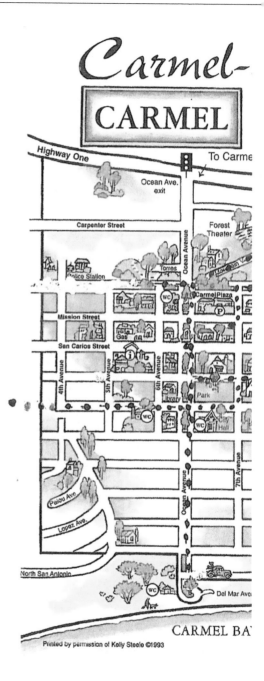

GNOME HOME

CARMEL BAY

by-the-Sea

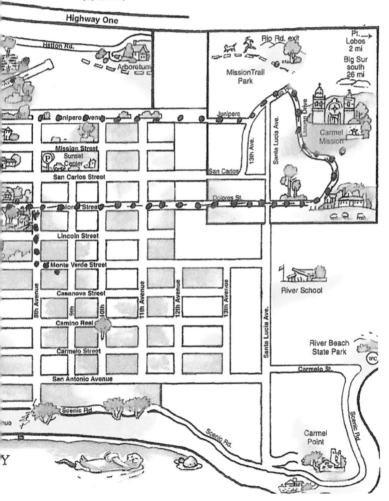

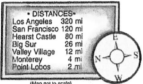

• DISTANCES•
Los Angeles 320 mi
San Francisco 120 mi
Hearst Castle 80 mi
Big Sur 26 mi
Valley Village 12 mi
Monterey 4 mi
Point Lobos 2 mi

(Map not to scale)

Highway One

Hatton Rd.

Arboretum

Rio Rd. exit

MissionTrail
Park

Pt.
Lobos
2 mi

Big Sur
south
26 mi

Junipero Avenue

Junipero

Mission Street

Sunset
Center

San Carlos Street

San Carlos

Carmel
Mission

Dolores Street

Lincoln Street

Monte Verde Street

Casanova Street

Camino Real

Carmelo Street

San Antonio Avenue

8th Avenue

9th

10th

11th Avenue

12th Avenue

13th Avenue

13th Ave.

Santa Lucia Ave.

Lasuen Drive

River School

River Beach
State Park

WC

Carmelo St.

Scenic Rd.

Scenic Rd.

Scenic Rd.

Carmel
Point

Y

AUTHOR'S NOTE

Our dear friends Ann and John Gila-Firman of Palo Alto, as a prank, stole our gnome from the garden while Fred and I were vacationing in Europe, took photos of it around town and returned it. Upon our return there was a photo book in the mail with no identifiers.

Mystified, my husband called our local newspaper, *The Carmel Pine Cone*, and reported the incident, hoping to reveal the "culprits." Meanwhile our friends admitted the dastardly deed so the newspaper interviewed them to get the whole story.

The published article is included here. One night I could not sleep (caffeine-induced wakefulness), so I thought up verses to go with the photos and wrote them down the next morning.

My husband and I embellished the original gnome photos with others to catch additional notable sights in our beautiful village of Carmel-by-the-Sea.

Several years passed with the project on the back burner, and both John and my husband sadly died. I promised John in his last hours that I would publish the book and mention his primary role in its development...so here we are. Enjoy!

There was a couple, Ann and John,

Who went a-shopping around town.

They came upon a darling gnome

And knew at once he must come home.

M. Hummeliken was his name,
But shortly "Hum" his name became.

They built a roof o'er his head
And gave him table, chair and bed.
Hum had a special little house
All to himself...well, him and Mouse.

Hum was so happy in his cottage
Amid the flowers, trees and lot-age.

He stood in the garden every night

Holding lantern, shedding light.

Hum lit the path so all could see -

Fairies, elves, and you and me.

Each evening he'd come alive
And sneak on up the cottage drive.

He'd peek in windows to make sure
His kind folks Ann and John were near,
Snuggled soundly in their bed
Asleep and dreaming with no dread.

And THEN upon one midnight clear

He found his dear folks were not here!

Where is Ann and where is John?

Where, oh where, could they have gone?

He questioned goose
and questioned gander.
Neither understood his dander.

Hum paced and paced, to and fro,

Then knew to village he must go

To look for them in lots of places

They often went and showed their faces.

Off he went, with duffle packed

To find his family and bring them back!

He crossed the bridge where lived the troll...

Hum held his breath, so brave of soul.

Knees were knocking as he scurried.

He sang loud as if not worried..

"Hi, ho, tiddly dee dum...

I'm not afraid of what will come!"

He made it safely to the town -

First to the beach by going down.

He stood upon the warming sand,

But could not see them, John and Ann.

Way up he climbed to Hansel, Gretel...

The hill began to test his mettle!

He spoke with other elves he found.

They shrugged, cast glances to the ground.

Then down to Tuck Box, Twigery too.

But no one had seen either through.

They could only extend to him

Best Wishes in his search for kin.

The Cypress Inn,

Where dogs would meet,

Offered a chair to rest his feet.

The jolly cafe Cottage bunch

Could only offer him a lunch.

Cottage of Sweets provided some fudge

Spurring him on to continue his trudge.

On to historic Golden Bough -
Plays and magic they endow.
Surely they had seen the two,
Who sometimes were on stage to view.

Alas, no luck was found there either
"To be or not to be"… just me there.

The sheep of Mission Ranch did bleat

Their main concern was counting feet.

They never looked above the knee,

So how would sheep know where they be?

Around the corner was the Mission
With a fountain and real fish-in.
Outside the vestibule Hum saw
Only crows gathered there to caw.

He tossed his last coin in the fountain,
Wishing magic he could count on.

"Ah, Forest Theater!" Hum did think,

Determined, though his cheeks were pink.

He climbed his way through hill and dale.

By now his cheeks had turned all pale.

Upon the stage all alone Hum stood.

He climbed the seats as best he could.

But alas, no fam-i-ly was there.
Poor little Hum did feel despair.

With heavy foot he trudged toward home,

Now unconcerned with troll, this gnome.

A tear was rolling down his cheek,

The outlook for his future..BLEAK.

His happy home had now become

A lonely shell - Hum felt all numb.

As he approached the house defeated,

He knew how fortunately treated

He had been with Ann and John -

Now lost for good, alone, abandoned.

WAIT! He heard strange sounds, loud voices!

Coming from his cottage - noises?

Hum hurried up the drive to view

His dear folk crying, "Oh, what to do!"

Their gnome was missing, they did wail.

He saw their cheeks were also pale.

He realized how loved he was!

His heart was pounding just because.

Hum rushed to show them, there he stood,

That he was back and safe in wood!

They hugged and kissed and swore to tell
When either ventured beyond their dell.

Never again to leave home alone,
Together forever,
John, Ann, and gnome!

This book is dedicated to my dear friends
Ann Gila and her husband John Firman,
inspirations in my life, and to my husband
Fred Nelson, who brought my gnome home.

THE TRUE STORY

As it appeared in **The Carmel Pine Cone,**
May 24, 2002

'GNOME ALONE' SEARCHES VILLAGE FOR MISSING FAMILY by Tamara Grippi

Karyl Hall and Fred Nelson returned home from a month's vacation in the south of France to discover that while they were gone, their 3-foot-tall garden gnome went on an adventure of his own.

The gnome was safely where he had always been – just outside a small cottage in their garden. But a mysterious package waiting at the post office contained a photo album that showed him on a remarkable trip around town – to the Lincoln Street footpath, the Forest Theater, Mission Ranch, and even Carmel Beach.

Hall and Nelson were delighted, but mystified as to who might have aided their small friend. "It was so funny and so clever," said Nelson. "But we couldn't get anybody to confess."

The couple's little companion, who is usually seen holding a lantern and beckoning visitors to their miniature elf cottage on Pescadero Road, apparently was lonesome and went looking for Hall and Nelson at some of their favorite Carmel haunts.

"Where is Karyl? Where is Fred?" the photo album asked on the first page, showing a snapshot of the white-bearded gnome decked out in his tall red elf cap, knocking on the front door of the couple's home.

The album's next few pages reveal photos of the little guy searching for the couple around their garden, peeking in windows and even looking perplexed in their empty gazebo.

The story continues to unfold as the pictures show the little gnome with his satchel tied around his waist setting out on a journey to find his lost friends. The lonely dwarf slowly made his way down Pescadero Road and across the Lincoln Street footbridge.

The next snapshot reveals an emboldened gnome approaching some of Carmel's well-known restaurants, also the favorites of Hall and Nelson – The Forge in the Forest, the Cottage, the Tuck Box and La Boheme.

Thwarted in these attempts, the little explorer takes his quest to a larger venue – the Forest Theater. The next few pictures show a determined gnome entering the gates of a deserted parking lot, looking out from an empty bench and finally taking center stage with his outstretched arm creating a dramatic gesture worthy only of a gnome.

Thence to Mission Ranch
From there, he is pictured on a lounge at Mission Ranch, gazing at the meadow. Finally, perhaps inevitably, the gnome finds himself at Carmel Beach, a wistful little traveler all alone on the stretches of white sand.

The last page of the picture album reads: "Gnome Alone, still."

Hall and Nelson were captivated with the book. "It was wonderful," Hall said. "The first time we opened it, we just laughed and laughed."
With the gnome safely back in front of his elf cottage, Hall and Nelson had no idea who accompanied their elfin friend on his journey.

Finally, four days after they returned home, they received a Federal Express mailing that revealed two of their friends happily hanging out with the gnome on the Lincoln Street footbridge.

Ann Gila and John Firman of Palo Alto had masterminded the whole plot. Gila and Firman spared no trouble to pull off their feat and they relished every minute.

Gila explained that the gnome's adventure was inspired by the plot of the random acts of kindness movie, "Amelie." In that film, the main character, Amelie, induces her father to travel by giving his gnome to a travel agent friend, who sends back pictures of the gnome at the Taj Mahal and numerous other famous places around the world.

For Hall and Nelson, who adored the movie, the gnome adventure was especially charming.

And Gila and Firman couldn't have had more fun carrying out their plan. "It was on a Monday, so it was fairly quiet in Carmel," Gila said. "I would double park and then my husband would jump out of the car with the gnome."

Somehow, they managed to avoid suspicion. Nothing showed up in the police log.

After Gila and Firman put the book together, Firman took a late-night ride on his motorcycle from Palo Alto back to Carmel just to make sure the package's postmark wouldn't identify them as the culprits.

"It was late on Friday night and he was wearing black leather and riding a Harley Davidson and delivering a package with no return address on it," Gila said. He was afraid someone would think he was a terrorist.

But even after all the pains to keep the gnome intrigue secret, Firman and Gila finally decided to confess by sending the "calling card" photograph showing them on the quest with the gnome.

Before their next vacation, Hall and Nelson said they'll be sure to let the gnome know where they're going and when they'll be back.

To benefit our community,
the profits from the sale of this
book go to our wonderful
local professional
Pacific Repertory Theatre
(PacRep), which performs
at the historic
Golden Bough
and Forest Theater.

CPSIA information can be obtained
at www.ICGtesting.com
Printed in the USA
FSOW04n0639201117
41252FS